COLORADO
A PHOTOGRAPHIC PORTFOLIO

CARR CLIFTON
Maroon Bells and Maroon Bells Lake,
Maroon Bells/Snowmass Wilderness White River National Forest

COLORADO

A PHOTOGRAPHIC PORTFOLIO

BROWNTROUT PUBLISHERS, INC.
SAN FRANCISCO

WILLARD CLAY
Monkey flower along Fraser Creek,
White River National Forest, Flat Tops Wilderness

COLORADO: A PHOTOGRAPHIC PORTFOLIO
features the finest photographs of Colorado by a
distinguished group of landscape photographers. Captions
for the photographs were provided by the photographers.

Photographs, Captions © 1995
Denver A. Bryan, Willard Clay, Carr Clifton,
Kathleen Norris Cook, Terry Donnelly, Jack W. Dykinga,
Dennis Flaherty, Jeff Foott, Fred Hirschmann,
George H. H. Huey, Barbara Magnuson, David Muench,
Marc Muench, Steve Mulligan, James Randklev,
Galen Rowell/Mountain Light, Tom Till, Larry Ulrich

LIBRARY OF CONGRESS
CATALOGING-IN-PUBLICATION DATA

Colorado, a photographic portfolio.
    p.   cm.
  ISBN 1-56313-616-3 (hardcover : alk. paper)
  ISBN 1-56313-758-5 (softcover : alk. paper)
   1. Colorado—Pictorial works.
F777.C63 1995   95-18913
978.8—dc20   CIP

Printed and bound by
Dai Nippon Printing Company, Ltd., Hong Kong

10 9 8 7 6 5 4 3 2

THE PHOTOGRAPHS

DAVID MUENCH
Sunflowers, Great Sand Dunes National Monument

INTRODUCTION

THE landscape photographer in Colorado today is working within a grand tradition. Just as William Henry Jackson's photographs of the Yellowstone area in the 1860s led to the establishment of the world's first national park and Ansel Adams' and Eliot Porter's images of wilderness inspired the environmental movement of the middle twentieth century, the photographs in this book can affect the way that people see the natural world and can help build a new movement for its preservation.

Each of the artists included in this volume have themselves been changed by the awesome power of the photographic image. Most are established professionals whose work appears in all the appropriate commercial and artistic settings. Their restless wanderings often take

them to the heart of the Rocky Mountains of North America in Colorado where that mighty range reaches above 14,000 feet and looms over the western extension of the Great Plains. All would agree that Colorado affords them profoundly moving scenes which they take as their task to capture and interpret.

But the camera is a tool not merely of observation but also of creation. Where the tired or indifferent traveler sees only dust and the slanting light of afternoon, the sensitive observer combines these elements into a beautiful representation of the passage of time and the suspension of the earthbound in the formless air. Without the artist the moment slips unrecorded into the infinite void. Indeed, it can be claimed that in an artless world both time and

history dissolve into nothingness since there would be no medium to sustain those temporal delusions.

The grandeur of Colorado's natural landscape defies the writer's ability to describe it because the conventional store of adjectives and superlatives is inadequate to the task. The skilled and patient photographer, by contrast, can ally himself with the powers of nature itself. Given enough time, the moon will rise, the mist will clear, the shadows will climb the canyon walls. And each passing minute recreates the world in ways that no one could imagine. That is why photography done well is so surprising—it shows us what we have *not* seen before, even in places we have been all of our lives. This is the Colorado we have sought to portray in this book.

TERRY DONNELLY
*Fresh snow on pines in the Collegiate Peaks Wilderness,
San Isabel National Forest*

JACK DYKINGA
Lupine and Indian paintbrush flowering in meadow with aspens at dawn, Rio Grande National Forest

DAVID MUENCH
Huron Peak top, Collegiate Peaks Wilderness

DENVER BRYAN
Mule deer bucks

LARRY ULRICH
Lower Blue Lake from Blue Lakes Pass, Mt. Sneffels Wilderness,
Uncompahgre National Forest, San Juan Mountains
17

FRED HIRSCHMANN
Morning light illuminating monoliths and spires,
Colorado National Monument

KATHLEEN NORRIS COOK
San Juan Mountains near Corkscrew Pass

LARRY ULRICH
Sneezeweed, West Elk Mountains,
Gunnison National Forest

JACK W. DYKINGA
Prairie sunflowers on the dunes,
Great Sand Dunes National Monument

WILLARD CLAY
Sunset light on Longs Peak and Trail Ridge,
Rocky Mountain National Park

JACK W. DYKINGA
Fireweed in bloom, Grand Mesa National Forest

TOM TILL
Wet sand, Great Sand Dunes National Monument

CARR CLIFTON
Fall-colored aspens,
Maroon Bells/Snowmass Wilderness,
White River National Forest

LARRY ULRICH
Yellow pond lilies, Molas Divide,
San Juan National Forest

DAVID MUENCH
Sprague Lake sunrise,
Rocky Mountain National Park

TOM TILL
Evening, Monument Canyon, Colorado National Monument

TERRY DONNELLY
Sculpted rocks above the Lincoln Creek Grottos, White River National Forest

GEORGE H. H. HUEY
Sunset, Blue Mesa Lake,
Curecanti National Recreation Area

GEORGE H. H. HUEY
Rocky Mountain bee plant growing on the edge of the dunes,
Great Sand Dunes National Monument

DAVID MUENCH
Winter transition, snow carpet in Dallas Divide, southwest Colorado

DENVER A. BRYAN
Pronghorn antelope fawn, one day old and exhibiting "still behavior" to avoid danger

JACK W. DYKINGA
Aspens surround pond atop mesa,
Grand Mesa National Forest

BARBARA MAGNUSON
Mountain goat nannies running across ridge,
Mount Evans, Arapahoe National Forest